MW00612615

Introduction to

The Believer's Authority

What you didn't learn in church

Andrew Wommack

© Copyright 2023 – Andrew Wommack

Printed in the United States of America. All rights reserved. No portion of this book may be reproduced, stored in a retrieval system, or transmitted in any form or by any means—electronic, mechanical, photocopy, recording, scanning, or other—except for brief quotations in critical reviews or articles, without the prior written permission of the publisher.

Unless otherwise indicated, all Scripture quotations are taken from the King James Version® of the Bible. Copyright © by the British Crown. Public domain.

All emphasis within Scripture quotations is the author's own.

Published in partnership between Andrew Wommack Ministries and Harrison House Publishers.

Woodland Park, CO 80863 – Shippensburg, PA 17257

ISBN 13 TP: 978-1-59548-589-2

For Worldwide Distribution, Printed in the USA

1 2 3 4 5 6 / 26 25 24 23

Contents

Introduction

I usually go out in the crowd an hour before each of my services and visit with people. I'd say that gives me a pretty good idea of what people are dealing with. I've heard it all, and the number one mistake I see people making is due to them not understanding their authority in Christ.

James 4:7b says, *"Resist the devil, and he will flee from you."* Yet the average believer is asking God or me to do what the Lord told them to do. We have to resist the devil, and he will flee from us. People know that God *can* do anything; they believe He has the power to do something, but they don't realize He has *already* done it. They just approach God like a beggar and say, "Oh God, would you please do this?" Then, if they don't see the results, they take it personally—like God has not found them worthy.

1

Another thing they will do is pray but not act on their faith. I couldn't tell you how many times I've had people tell me that they're just "waiting on God" to do something.

Maybe you're feeling stuck. Maybe you've been taught to "wait on the Lord" and you're just not seeing His will come to pass in your life. If you are experiencing resistance to what God called you to do in ministry, business, or any other area of life, I want you to know that He has given you authority through Jesus Christ to make a way where there doesn't seem to be a way—to move the mountains that are hindering you from success.

I'm going to be sharing with you some of the most foundational things that God has ever shown me, and I guarantee you this is going to rub religion the wrong way. I am not against true Christianity. I am a believer, and I know the church is God's agent here on the earth. But so much of religion today, even what is called Christian religion, is not preaching and proclaiming the truth. It has taught people that God just sovereignly controls things in a way that takes away any responsibility we have to use our authority.

Many Christians just don't understand that God has delegated authority to us, and it's not God who's letting the devil ruin people's lives. It's us. We're the ones with power and authority, and we're the ones who have empowered the devil.

In this booklet, I'll be sharing some things that, I can guarantee you, are going to be contrary to a lot of the things that you've heard. But if you can receive it, it will help you.

I can truthfully say that, of all the things that I've seen God do in my life, this is one of the most important things that he's shown me. We are in a spiritual battle and, as believers, we have authority.

Satan Has No Power of His Own

Finally, my brethren, be strong in the Lord, and in the power of his might. Put on the whole armour of God, that ye may be able to stand against the wiles of the devil.

Ephesians 6:10–11

Notice that word *wiles*. According to *Vine's Expository Dictionary*, it means "cunning, craftiness, and deception."[1] In other words, it means "lies." Satan doesn't have any power of his own. One of the things I'm going to explain is where Satan got his power from. He did not get it from God. I know you might be thinking, *Well, where did he get it from?*

He got it from you and me. I know that may be a shock, but I hope you don't just close this booklet before you give me an opportunity to explain. Satan's only real weapon against you is deception. And renewing your mind (Rom. 12:2) to the Word of God will defeat deception. The power of deception is completely broken once you know the truth. This is the reason Jesus said in John 8:32, you *"shall know the truth, and the truth shall make you free."* But it's only the truth you *know* that makes you free. This is speaking about more than intellectual knowledge. It is an experiential knowing, like when Adam "knew" Eve, and they had a child as a result (Gen. 4:1). It is intimacy that only comes with experience.

Jesus stated (John 17:17) that when we are set apart and understand the truth of His Word in an intimate, experiential way, then we will be delivered from all of our bondage.

I think the believer's authority is one of the least understood things among Christians. That's because many Christians just haven't made themselves intimately aware of the truth, and that's what has kept them in bondage to Satan's lies. I was raised in a church that taught us to believe that all the demons were in some third-world country—certainly not in America. But anyone who is spiritually aware knows that there is demonic activity anywhere you go. We just tend to look at things on the surface level and don't see that the origin of many things that happen on a daily basis—things that tick us off and come against us—is spiritual. We fail to recognize the spiritual

> **Satan's only real weapon against you is deception.**

influence behind things. That's why we need to be on guard against Satan's lies and stand on the truth of God's Word.

Who Made Satan?

Most Christians believe the answer to this question is obvious. "God created Satan," they might say. But that's not really true. God created Lucifer. That may seem like a small distinction at first glance, but once you understand who really made Satan, it will change your perspective of him forever.

I believe God created everything, including Lucifer. He was created as a powerful anointed angel. Ezekiel 28:13–14 says that Lucifer was in the Garden of Eden, that *"every precious stone"* was his covering, that musical instruments (*"tabrets"* and *"pipes"*) were put on the inside of him, and that he was an *"anointed cherub."* (A cherub isn't a chubby baby with a little bow and arrow, like you might see in popular art; cherubim are huge and mighty warrior angels.) Lucifer was even *"upon the holy mountain of God."* But he wasn't satisfied with that, and he didn't remain the anointed cherub that God created him to be.

Most people believe that Lucifer took one-third of the angels and rebelled against God in heaven, where he was defeated and then cast to earth. This is all taken from one scripture, Revelation 12:4 (*"his tail drew the third part of the stars of heaven, and did cast them to the earth"*), which is allegorical. It's not a good idea to base any belief on a single scripture (Deut. 17:6, Matt. 18:16, and 2 Cor. 13:1); and even if one-third of the angels rebelled against God, He still would have prevailed if *100 percent* of the angels rebelled!

I believe Satan was originally on this earth in the Garden of Eden as Lucifer. He was God's angel sent to earth to be a blessing to Adam and Eve. Hebrews 1:14 says, *"Are they not all ministering spirits, sent forth to minister for them who shall be heirs of salvation?"* Lucifer wasn't sent to the earth to tempt Adam and Eve but to bless them. He was an angelic being sent to be their protector, to minister to them, and to serve them. He was there on a divine mission, still in his perfect state. It was in the garden that his transgression against God was conceived and carried out.

Ezekiel 28:15 goes on to say, *"Thou wast perfect in thy ways from the day that thou wast created, till iniquity was found in thee."*

Now, I've never been able to follow the logic that God sent Satan to earth to tempt man and see how he would respond. As a parent, would you send your children out into the backyard to play if there were lions or bears there? That would be irresponsible. The Father wouldn't do that to us, and he didn't do that to Adam and Eve. So, what made Lucifer turn against God? Lucifer watched as God did something for man that He had never done with any other of His creation. When God created man, not only was he made in the very image of God, but he was then given unconditional authority over this earth.

Dominion Given to Man

God created man in his own image, in the image of God created he him; male and female created he them. And God blessed them, and God said unto them, Be fruitful, and multiply, and replenish the earth, and subdue it: and have dominion over the fish of the sea, and over the fowl of the air, and over every living thing that moveth upon the earth.

Genesis 1:27–28

Notice God didn't say to them, "Now as long as you follow my leading and as long as you do what I want you to do, I will let you have dominion over the earth." There was zero qualification for this power and authority. God spoke it and that was it.

In Psalm 89:34, God says, *"My covenant will I not break, nor alter the thing that is gone out of my lips."* So, when God created and blessed mankind, He gave His word on it. God cannot lie. It's the integrity of His Word that holds the entire universe together (Heb. 1:3). All throughout the first chapter of Genesis, God spoke things into being. Hebrews 11:3 says, *"the worlds were framed by the word of God."*

Unlike human beings who may change their minds, God will not violate His Word. When He told Adam and Eve they had dominion, authority, and power to subdue and rule, it was done. If you're familiar with the third chapter of Genesis, you might be thinking, *But Satan deceived them! Shouldn't God have stopped him?* When Adam and Eve fell, God couldn't just say, "Time out! King's X! Do over!"

No! Once God says something, that's it. He can't go back on it.

Now, Lucifer understood the integrity of God's words, and when he heard this, I believe his antenna went up. He saw that Adam and Eve had something he wanted but didn't have—they had unconditional authority. In a way, they had been made the gods of this world; it was theirs to rule and subdue.

Psalm 115:16 says, *"The heaven, even the heavens, are the LORD's: but the earth hath he given to the children of men."*

You see, even though Lucifer may have been God's number one angel, he still wanted more. He was jealous and envious. Isaiah 14:13–14 says,

> *For thou hast said in thine heart, I will ascend into heaven, I will exalt my throne above the stars of God: I will sit also upon the mount of the congregation, in the sides of the north. I will ascend above the heights of the clouds; I will be like the most High.*

Lucifer didn't hate God—he was jealous of God. He wanted to take God's place. Through man, Lucifer saw that he could have authority and power that he didn't already have.

God of This World

When God gave Adam and Eve authority, that meant He was no longer in direct control. He could only function in this world through people because John 4:24 says, *"God is a Spirit."* He's not a physical being. Lucifer realized this, which is why he didn't attack God directly. See, Satan is stupid, but he's not ignorant. As I said earlier, he couldn't have taken down God with 100 percent of the angels in heaven, much less one third. So, he went after mankind instead, choosing to attack Eve first. I believe that Lucifer came to the woman first because God told Adam not to eat of the fruit of the tree of the knowledge of good and evil (Gen. 2:16–17), before she was created (Gen. 2:22). That means that Eve didn't get the same command directly from God. She got it from Adam.

> Lucifer saw that he could have authority and power that he didn't already have.

Any time you get something through another person, that leaves the potential that maybe they didn't say it exactly the same way. Have you ever played the game where a story starts down at one end of the line and somebody whispers something to the next person? They're supposed to repeat the phrase exactly to the next person, but after it goes through five or six people, you can guarantee it's not going to be the same. There is just something that gets lost in transmission from person to person, and I believe the reason that Lucifer came to Eve is because she got information secondhand.

And the Lord God commanded the man, saying, Of every tree of the garden thou mayest freely eat: but of the tree of the knowledge of good and evil, thou shalt not eat of it: for in the day that thou eatest thereof thou shalt surely die.

Genesis 2:16–17

*And the woman said unto the serpent, We may eat of the fruit of the trees of the garden: but of the fruit of the tree which is in the midst of the garden, God hath said, Ye shall not eat of it, **neither shall ye touch it**, lest ye die.*

Genesis 3:2–3

Even though Eve was deceived, Adam knew what he was doing when he took the fruit and ate (1 Tim. 2:14). He heard the same things that Eve heard, but it didn't deceive him.

So, who made Satan? We did! The moment Adam and Eve yielded to Lucifer, he became Satan, the god of this world. In Romans 6:16, the apostle Paul wrote,

Know ye not, that to whom ye yield yourselves servants to obey, his servants ye are to whom ye obey; whether of sin unto death, or of obedience unto righteousness?

Lucifer understood that if he could deceive Adam and Eve into willingly relinquishing their authority to him that he could become the god of this world. He could take the authority that was given to mankind, use it to thwart the kingdom of God, and receive the praise, adoration, and glory he wanted.

Principalities, Powers, Rulers, and High Places

For we wrestle not against flesh and blood, but against principalities, against powers, against the rulers of the darkness of this world, against spiritual wickedness in high places.

Ephesians 6:12

Did you know that there are four things mentioned in this verse, and they're all related to the demonic? It's not really people who we're dealing with. It's Satan.

Although people may be the ones involved, it's actually demonic principalities, powers, rulers of darkness, and spiritual wickedness in high places working through them.

Back in 2009, we bought property in Woodland Park, Colorado, and for two and a half years, I tried to get the permits to start building our new Charis Bible College campus. We already had all the drawings done and were ready to go. But people just fought us on a lot of different things. We hired lawyers and went to local government meetings, but the opposition was just unbelievable.

So, I stood in faith. I was patient and praised God as I drove past that property every day. I spoke blessings over it and said we would get the permits and begin building. But after two and a half years—and I don't know why it took so long—I just got mad. I got a holy anger. I realized it wasn't just

> It's not really people who we're dealing with. It's Satan.

people that we were dealing with. It was the devil. And I got mad! Right then, I started yelling at the devil and telling him to get his hands off that property.

Now, I didn't wish anything bad to happen to those who were opposing us, but I declared that they were either going to get out of the way or they were going to get run over. And, in the name of Jesus, I commanded the demonic power that was hindering us to stop!

The next week we got the permit, praise the Lord! But I wondered why in the world it took me two and a half years to get angry enough over what the devil was doing to begin taking my authority. Just as there are authorities in the physical realm (human government), there are demonic authorities in the spiritual realm— and they are working against us. Once we realize we have authority in the spiritual realm, we can take back the ground Satan has stolen from us and remove any hindrances to God's plans in our lives.

Over the years, we've fought more battles over government lockdowns and resistance to expanding our Charis campus. But, praise God, I'm growing, and we are getting thing done! Even though I realize we have to do things in the natural and we have to deal with people, I'm no longer waiting to get on the devil's case and rebuke demonic opposition. I'm taking my authority over the demonic power that operates through people.

Beware of Your Enemy

If you don't yield yourself to Satan like Adam and Eve and give him authority in your life, you do not have to be afraid of him. But you do need to be aware. We need to be on guard. We don't need to be complacent. Colossians 2:8 says,

Beware lest any man spoil you through philosophy and vain deceit, after the tradition of men, after the rudiments of the world, and not after Christ.

That word *beware* is being used in the sense of a sentry on guard duty. It's a military term talking about being on guard or being on the lookout. And the word *spoil* is talking about the spoils of war that go to the victor—the gold, silver, and land. Paul was saying to be on guard, or you would be overcome by an enemy that will strip you of your treasure, which is the truth that God has placed in your heart. That enemy, Satan, wants to steal what God has given to you by using the world's philosophies and the religious traditions of man.

Religious tradition says that God is sovereign, that He controls everything. It says that nothing happens but what God allows. Some even say that Satan is like a dog on a leash—that he is allowed by God to put sickness and poverty on people.

No! That is just wrong, wrong, wrong. John 10:10 says, *"The thief [Satan] cometh not, but for to steal, and to kill, and to destroy."*

I believe the "sovereignty of God" is the worst doctrine in the church today. I know that this is a shocking statement and is near blasphemy to some people, but the way sovereignty is taught today is a real faith killer. The belief that God controls everything that happens to us is one of the devil's biggest inroads into our lives.

Satan is the one who is trying to steal from us, kill us, and destroy us. If we are not aware—if we allow ourselves to be deceived by the "tradition of men"— our enemy will take advantage and cause all sorts of mayhem.

During the war in Vietnam, I was stationed on a small fire-support base that was forty-one miles from the nearest U.S. military installation. A fire-support base is an isolated outpost that provides artillery support to soldiers in the field. I sometimes had to serve as a bunker guard. It was my duty to sit on top of that bunker and watch for potential attacks from the enemy. Some people didn't take guard duty seriously, and they would sleep through their whole shift, but I couldn't do that. We were in a war, and sleeping through guard duty put everyone's life at risk.

I spent my twenty-first birthday in Vietnam, and I actually took twenty-one direct hits on the bunker I was in, and I could see the muzzle fire from our enemies' weapons. On nights like that, I can guarantee you, nobody was sleeping on bunker duty. We took things seriously because we knew that the enemy was out there trying to kill us. Christians need to get the same sense of vigilance.

Get Angry at the Devil

Ephesians 4:26 says,

Be ye angry, and sin not: let not the sun go down upon your wrath.

That doesn't mean just get all of your wrath confessed before you go to bed at night. That means get angry and sin not. There is a righteous type of anger that you use against the devil, and you shouldn't ever put it to bed.

In James 4:7, the Bible says,

Submit yourselves therefore unto God. Resist the devil, and he will flee from you.

That word *resist* means to actively fight against. That's why you have to not let the sun set on your anger at the devil! Keep actively fighting against him! But why are we supposed to fight against the devil? Shouldn't God be fighting for us instead? Notice, James 4:7 says, *"he will flee from **you**."*

You see, there is no longer any direct conflict between God and the devil. Jesus already met the devil in battle, and He beat Satan hands down. Jesus took the keys of death and of hell (Rev. 1:18). He paraded the defeated Satan openly for all to see (Col. 2:15). Jesus is Lord, amen!

The devil doesn't flee from God directly. But God shared His authority with you and me. So, even though Satan isn't directly fighting against God, he is coming against you and me with wiles, lies, and deceptions (Eph. 6:11). Satan is fighting you, me, and other believers. We have to take our authority and resist the devil so he will flee from us.

One time, I was ministering to a person who had just been serving the devil and gave him a huge inroad into their life. I said, "I can cast this devil out, but unless you are in agreement with me, this thing will come back seven times worse (Matt. 12:45). You have to *resist* the devil!"

We knelt around a coffee table, and I said, "I want you to tell the devil that you are taking back ground, that you repent, and that you are no longer going to live this way. I want you to talk to the devil and resist him, and then I'll pray and cast this demon out." So, this person starts out saying, "Dear devil...," and I had to stop them right there and minister some correction. Saying, "Dear devil, please leave me alone," is not resisting the devil. No, you aren't supposed to approach him that way. You need to get angry!

God gave us the ability to get angry. The sad fact is most of us use it against people. We aren't supposed to be angry at people, though. We need to be angry and sin not by directing it at the demonic power that operates *through* people. The fact is that people are being influenced, controlled, and used by the devil to hinder what God called us to do.

Now, you may be thinking, *Are people possessed, oppressed, or depressed?* I believe it's useless to debate that. In the Greek, where the Bible says a person was demon possessed, the word literally means *demonized*. It just means they were under the control of the devil. Christianity has tried to make something out of possessed, oppressed, or depressed. But it's not in Scripture.

You just keep your anger focused on the devil and use it against him instead of people!

Satan Uses People

I get a lot of criticism because of the truths I share. There was a time when I took things personally and thought, *Why is this person so upset with me?* I just tried to deal with them on the natural level.

Since then, I've come to recognize that Satan is the one who's trying to get my attention off what God has told me to do. I recognize that the enemy is using some person to come against me. I've even had some good friends come against me, but I've been able to forgive them. I recognized that they had a sensitivity in some area that Satan took advantage of and used against me. Because I look beyond the person and don't take their comments personally, I'm able to put things into perspective and deal with it.

Years ago, there was a minister who told people to burn my teaching materials and that I was the slickest cult leader they'd seen since Jim Jones. What they said didn't bless me, but I didn't let that stop me from blessing them. I even gave money to their ministry. Years later, we shared the stage on a Christian television show and got to know each other to the place we've since become friends. That wouldn't have happened if I had taken their criticism personally and fought against them. It was the devil that came against me through that person. I took my authority over the devil and kept preaching the Gospel and didn't take it personally. I'm not going to yield myself to Satan, get in strife, and open the door for him to work in my life.

If you had a biblical mindset, it would make a huge difference in how you respond to people in difficult situations. You'd recognize that it's not that person who sits next to you at work; it's not really your neighbor, your spouse, or your circumstances that are coming against you. They can be influenced, inspired, and used by Satan, but they aren't really the source. When you genuinely understand that it isn't a physical battle, it changes the way you respond.

Jesus exemplified this same perspective. He recognized when the devil was trying to get to Him through a person.

After Peter—under the influence of God—confessed Jesus as *"the Christ, the Son of the living God"* (Matt. 16:16), the Lord explained to His disciples about His coming crucifixion, death, and resurrection. Peter responded, *"Be it far from thee, Lord: this shall not be unto thee"* (Matt. 16:22). Apparently, Peter had missed Jesus saying He would rise again on the third day. Peter didn't even want to consider the thought of Him being taken and killed.

Jesus said to Peter in Matthew 16:23,

Get thee behind me, Satan: thou art an offence unto me: for thou savourest not the things that be of God, but those that be of men.

Jesus recognized that Satan was speaking through Peter. There are times when the devil speaks through people to get at you. Of course, they may be unaware they're being used by Satan. Peter was probably shocked, hurt, and offended when Jesus turned around and said, "Get behind me, Satan!" However, there are times when you need to rebuke the devil that way too.

Rebuking Unbelief

When our oldest son Joshua was one year old, my mother invited us to go on a vacation to the Smoky Mountains. Jamie and I didn't have any money, so she offered to pay for everything.

Now, my mother had just started trying to believe God for healing, but when she tried to resist a cold and it didn't work, she got discouraged. When we started traveling with our son, she said, "Keep him away from me. He's going to catch my cold, and he'll be sick."

We didn't believe in that. We believed in healing and that our son wouldn't get sick, so I just politely said, "He's going to be fine. He will not catch your cold. In the name of Jesus, he's healed."

But my mother just kept speaking negatively during that trip. For example, she said, "We don't have money to do this," and I said, "If you don't have the money, let's turn around now because I don't have any money, and I can't help you." She said, "Oh, I've got plenty of money," but she was just being negative.

When our son sat in front of the air conditioner, she said, "Oh, he'll catch a cold." And I said, "He's not going to catch a cold." Every time she'd say something negative, I'd counter it and try to speak the opposite.

On the first night of our trip, we stopped at a hotel and all stayed in the same room. We had a little crib for Joshua. At about 11 p.m., Joshua woke up with this croup in his throat that you could have heard in the next room. So, I got up and prayed in tongues over him, rebuked the coughing, spoke healing, and he was fine within about twenty minutes. I laid down Joshua and went back to bed, but thirty minutes later he woke up again coughing.

I did that like a yo-yo, getting up and laying down, until two or three in the morning.

Finally, one time on my way back to bed after I had put Joshua back to sleep, I heard my mother say, "Admit it, Andy. He's sick!" So, I got right down in her face and said, "Satan, in the name of Jesus, I bind your confession. I refuse to listen to your unbelief. My son will not be sick. I reject everything you're saying!"

Joshua didn't wake up again that night, he never got sick, and my mother didn't speak to me for two days! We were on vacation, just having a wonderful time, and she wouldn't talk at all.

When my mother finally did speak, she said, "I'm sorry you think I'm the devil!" So, I told her, "Mother, you know I don't think you're the devil, but that was the devil speaking through you."

I'm not saying that we're only in a spiritual battle. There is also a physical battle. There is demonic opposition, and it flows through people. There are times that we have to stand up and speak to people, and there are times that we have to fight against demonic influences.

Words Have Power

And on the morrow, when they were come from Bethany, he was hungry: and seeing a fig tree afar off having leaves, he came, if haply he might find any thing thereon: and when he came to it, he found nothing but leaves; for the time of figs was not yet. And Jesus answered and said unto it, No man eat fruit of thee hereafter for ever. And his disciples heard it.

Mark 11:12–14

Jesus was hungry, and He saw a fig tree. It had leaves, but no figs. Because it had no figs, He cursed it! Now, what was going on here?

You see, in Israel, a fig tree produces figs at the same time or before it produces leaves. If a fig tree has leaves, it's supposed to have figs. Jesus saw that this fig tree had leaves. It wasn't time for figs yet, but it wasn't time for leaves either. He was going to get some figs and eat them. But when he got there, there were no figs.

This tree was out of order. Jesus just spoke to it and said, *"No man eat fruit of thee hereafter for ever."* And the Bible made special mention that *"his disciples heard it."* They took note that He had talked to this fig tree. Then, they all went on into Jerusalem (Mark 11:15–16).

Jesus cast the money changers out of the temple, overturned their tables, and then they went back to where He was staying in Bethany. The Gospel of Mark doesn't say, but it's implied that Jesus and the disciples went back the same way later that day and they didn't notice any difference in this fig tree. But in verse 20 of that same chapter, it says,

> *And in the morning, as they passed by, they saw the fig tree dried up from the roots.*

Now, that is amazing!

Jesus spoke to the fig tree the day before as they were entering into Jerusalem, and the next day it was *"dried up from the roots."* That's really significant! That means the moment Jesus spoke to the fig tree, it was dead. But it took about twenty-four hours for what happened below the surface to manifest above the surface.

There are so many applications of this. At the very moment you speak to a situation—a sickness in your body, poverty, or something else—and believe with all of your heart and doubt not, you receive. But you have to believe that you receive when you *pray*, not when you see it. That's when you shall *have* it, and you shall *see* it later on.

In Mark 11:20–21 it says, "*And in the morning, as they passed by, they saw the fig tree dried up from the roots. And Peter calling to remembrance saith unto him, Master, behold, the fig tree which thou cursedst is withered away.*"

Jesus was about to teach His disciples a key principle on how to use authority.

Speak to Your Mountain

Jesus had just spoken to the fig tree. He didn't use an axe, salt the ground, or do anything in the natural. He just spoke, and it died. And the next day, it was completely dead. The disciples were shocked! They were amazed at the power and authority that Jesus had.

And then Jesus answered, *"Have faith in God. For verily I say unto you, That whosoever shall say unto this mountain, Be thou removed, and be thou cast into the sea; and shall not doubt in his heart, but shall believe that those things which he saith shall come to pass; he shall have whatsoever he saith"* (Mark 11:22–23).

The words *"say"* and *"saith"* are used four times. Jesus emphasized that the way to use authority is through your words. God Almighty used words to create the world (Heb. 11:3). Words are a powerful force, and we've got to understand that everything in the natural realm responds to words. Sad to say, most Christians speak to God about their mountain instead of speaking to their mountain about God! The mountain represents whatever your problem is. Jesus declared, "Speak to your mountain, and command it to be cast into the sea!" The average Christian prays, "God, I have this mountain. Would You please move it for me?" This kind of prayer isn't helpful. The Lord told you to talk to *it*, not to Him. Whatever it is, speak to it! This is a truth about authority that most people miss.

One time, Charles Capps was in the midst of a prayer when the Lord said to him, "What are you doing?" Charles responded, "I'm praying." But the Lord corrected him by saying, "No, you're not. You're complaining!"[2]

> **Jesus emphasized that the way to use authority is through your words.**

I want you to know the purpose of prayer is not to inform "poor, misinformed" God about your problems. We need to recognize that God already knows our every need (Matt. 6:8) and has already made provision for them "*according to his riches in glory by Christ Jesus*" (Phil. 4:19).

God can do *"exceeding abundantly above all that we ask or think"* (Eph. 3:20), but that's not the end of that verse. Most people think it stops right there, but the apostle Paul also wrote *"according to the power that worketh in us."* As believers, we have power—raising from the dead power (Eph. 1:20)—on the inside of us, and we release that power by exercising authority with our words!

The whole thing that caused Jesus to tell us to speak to our mountain was the fig tree that spoke to Him through its leaves in Mark 11:13. Jesus spoke back to the fig tree, and it obeyed His command. Sometimes circumstances speak to us. Sometimes our body speaks to us through symptoms, or our wallet speaks to us when we're called to give and have a stack of bills in front of us. When this happens, we need to follow Jesus' example, and use the authority God has given us.

Talk Back to Your Problems

If anything talks to you, you need to talk back to it. If something speaks to me, and it's something contrary to the Word of God, I talk to it. And I specifically talk back to television and radio.

When the news says it's flu season and that you're going to get sick because the weather has changed, I'll talk back to it. When the news tells me that we're in a recession and that we can't expand, I'll talk back to it.

I remember when the so-called "Great Recession" happened in 2008, God told me that we needed to start expanding our Bible college. In the Colorado Springs area where our ministry was located at the time, there were hundreds of Christian nonprofit organizations. During that same time, many of those ministries started planning for a decreased income. They cut their bud-

> If something speaks to me, and it's something contrary to the Word of God, I talk to it.

gets significantly. I knew many of these ministers personally, so I heard about these things. When I heard people talking about how they were cutting back and decreasing, I would counter it by saying, "Not me! My

God supplies *all of* [my] *need according to his riches in glory by Christ Jesus"* (Phil. 4:19).

I made some very bold, God-inspired predictions. I didn't know the details, the difficulties we would face, or the exact cost, but I went on record and said that we were going to build to accommodate growth. Instead of cutting back, we were going to expand. We simply refused to participate in the recession, amen!

At about that time, we bought property up the road in Woodland Park and began the largest expansion and increase of expenses in our ministry up to that time. And because of the things that I spoke, in nine years, we produced $130 million worth of property and buildings—and we did it debt free! There were things that I did in the natural, like sharing God's vision on television and with our partners, but a lot of our success came from taking my authority and speaking against the negative things people were saying.

That recession was a mountain that I had to speak to. The news and experts tried to make it so big, they called it "Great." Instead of talking to the recession about their God, many Christians talked to God about the recession. Ministers of the Gospel were stopping God's vision from coming to pass by effectively saying to Him, "I know You said You'd supply all of my needs, but there's this recession."

It's important that, as believers, we not only confess the right things by saying what the Bible says about a situation, but we also have to guard against thoughts contrary to God's Word, so they do not become our words.

"Take No Thought, Saying"

Therefore take no thought, saying, What shall we eat? or, What shall we drink? or, Wherewithal shall we be clothed? (For after all these things do the Gentiles seek:) for your heavenly Father knoweth that ye have need of all these things. But seek ye first the kingdom of God, and his righteousness; and all these things shall be added unto you.

Matthew 6:31–33

Jesus said, *"take no thought, saying."* You may not be able to keep thoughts from coming to you, especially since we live in a world where we are flooded with negative information from the internet, television, and other media. But they don't become *your* thoughts until you say them. Kenneth E. Hagin described this concept by quoting an old saying: "You can't keep birds from flying overhead, but you can keep them from building a nest in your hair!"[3]

You can't necessarily keep all thoughts from coming at you because we live in a fallen world. Even if you turn off the television and avoid social media, well-meaning family and friends may share negative information with you. But you don't have to take those thoughts; and the way you keep from taking them is not to speak them.

The power of God is released through words. When you speak, if you believe what you say in your heart and don't doubt, you release this authority, and demonic powers will submit to you. But it is something that has to become a lifestyle. You have to train yourself to mean what you say.

Psalm 15:4 says a man who fears the Lord swears to his own hurt, and changes not. That means we follow through on our promises, even if it looks like it will benefit us nothing in the natural. Swearing to our own hurt and not changing is considered a godly characteristic. Keeping our word is the right thing to do, even when it isn't something we want to do.

If you are going to speak to things and see the authority of God released, you're going to have to start believing in the power of words. That means you quit breaking promises or saying things that are destructive to yourself and to others. Maybe you've heard some people say things like, "This tickles me to death," or "That scares me to death." The only reason they don't fall over when they say something like that is because they don't mean it. Romans 10:10 says you have to confess with your mouth *and* believe in your heart. But they're still training their hearts to disregard their own words because they just don't mean what they say.

You can't live all week long totally voiding your words, then speak and believe God when you come up against something. Your heart is going to go in the direction of your dominant thoughts. And if you live most of the time carnally and do not stand by your words, when something big comes up and you try and speak your faith, it's not going to work.

So, you can speak to your mountain with faith-filled words and remove obstacles that are keeping God's will from coming to pass. You can also rebuke Satan when he is working in people through unbelief. But how do you apply your authority when you are believing to influence someone else for God?

Interceding for Someone Else

We have power and authority in the spiritual realm, but we don't have authority over other people. You can't just pray and make other people do what you or God wants them to do. Specifically, you can't just pray and claim a person's salvation.

They can't get born again on your faith. God doesn't have any grandchildren. Every person has to have their own personal relationship with God. So, I want to show you how the authority of the believer works specifically in intercession for other people.

The very first thing I do when I intercede for others is I just remind myself of 2 Peter 3:9, which says,

The Lord is not slack concerning his promise, as some men count slackness; but is longsuffering to us-ward, not willing that any should perish, but that all should come to repentance.

Instead of going to God as if He's the problem, I start off by praising God (Ps. 100:4) for His goodness:

> **Your heart is going to go in the direction of your dominant thoughts.**

"Father, thank You that You're a good God. It's not Your fault that this person isn't born again. It's not You that hasn't saved them. You aren't willing that any should perish, but that all should come to repentance. Jesus, you've already died for this person (1 John 2:2). You want them born again more than I do."

In 2 Corinthians 4:4, the apostle Paul wrote,

In whom the god of this world [Satan] hath blinded the minds of them that believe not, lest the light of the glorious gospel of Christ, who is the image of God, should shine unto them.

So, you have to rebuke spiritual blindness, but then you also have to do something to get the truth to people. Jesus said in John 8:32,

And ye shall know the truth, and the truth shall make you free.

It's only the truth you know that makes you free.

A person can't come to the Lord just on their own. They have to be drawn by the Holy Spirit. Jesus said in John 6:44,

No man can come to me, except the Father which hath sent me draw him.

Also, people are *"born again, not of corruptible seed, but of incorruptible, by the word of God"* (1 Pet. 1:23).

The apostle Peter calls the Word of God a seed, like a sperm. The way that children are conceived is through a sperm being sown. In the same way, the Word of God is the sperm—the seed of God. This is how people are born again. They aren't born again by a virgin birth. Someone, somehow has to plant the seed of God's Word.

In Matthew 9:37–38, Jesus told His disciples,

The harvest truly is plenteous, but the labourers are few; Pray ye therefore the Lord of the harvest, that he will send forth labourers into his harvest.

I personally believe that you can't just substitute somebody else if you can go minister to them first. If at all possible, you need to put your feet to your prayers (Rom. 10:17). If for some reason you cannot reach that person, *then* you pray laborers across their path. You can also pray that God will bring seeds to remembrance that have already been sown—truths they've already heard. In John 14:26, Jesus said,

But the Comforter, which is the Holy Ghost, whom the Father will send in my name, he shall…bring all things to your remembrance, whatsoever I have said unto you.

Making a Difference

I remember one time in the army at Fort Dix, New Jersey, when I was waiting to get paid, it was cold outside. So, about forty of us were all huddled from the wind in a small structure, and we had to wait for about thirty minutes.

While we were there, one guy just got to blaspheming God and saying terrible things about Jesus. I was sitting there thinking, *Oh God, help me to make a difference in this situation.* At about the same time, that man stopped and said, "That's no way for a 'good old Scofield-Bible-carrying Baptist' to talk." So, I responded, "You ought to read it sometime. Haven't you ever read Matthew 12:36–37?"

But I say unto you, That every idle word that men shall speak, they shall give account thereof in the day of judgment. For by thy words thou

*shalt be justified, and by thy words thou shalt
be condemned.*

Boy, did he get mad! This guy started pushing his way through that crowd, and right about the time he got up to me, I said, "Here's one other scripture: Galatians 4:16":

*Am I therefore become your enemy, because I
tell you the truth?*

That guy was face to face with me, but he just stopped, turned his back, and never said another word. Here we were, all huddled together in total silence. There wasn't any more profanity, either! What I said changed the whole spiritual climate. In fact, for the next six weeks, not one word was spoken to me. When I'd walk into the barracks and everyone was cursing, they'd see me and just get totally quiet.

Later on, the man who was blaspheming God came to me and said, "Ever since you've talked to me, I haven't been able to sleep at night. I've been so convicted!" I came to find out that before he joined the army, this man had been singing in gospel music quartets and had even appeared on stage with a well-known group. But there he was saying all sorts of ungodly things about the Lord. Even though we parted ways before I could fully minister to him, I found out years later that he became a minister of the Gospel. Praise God!

Now, maybe I didn't do everything perfectly in that situation, but God used it. And what would have happened if I hadn't taken the authority God gave me? What would have become of that man?

Now, it's possible the seed of God's Word got on the inside of that man when he was singing in churches and my speaking boldly to him sparked something that allowed the Holy Spirit to bring scriptures to his remembrance. It's also possible I was the laborer someone else prayed across his path. Whatever the case, by taking my authority as a believer, I was able to make a difference for God.

We shouldn't be timid in situations where people are cursing, blaspheming, or performing all sorts of ungodly acts. As Christians, we're the ones who have been made righteous by Jesus Christ! It's all the other people who should be uncomfortable and not us. We need to start recognizing that we are the ones who are anointed, so we should exercise our authority and stand up to the devil!

Conclusion

You and I are in a spiritual battle. We have an enemy, and he is out to steal, kill, and destroy. Sad to say, most Christians don't realize they are being passive and letting Satan run all over them by allowing him to use the very authority God has given them. People are being taught that God just sovereignly controls things. They don't understand that God has delegated authority to us; it's not God who's letting the devil ruin people's lives. It's us!

The power of deception is completely broken once you know the truth. Satan has no power, except what he's taken from you. If you know the truth, any deception, any lie, any falsehood just loses its power. I can guarantee, these things may be contrary to a lot of what you've heard before. But, if you can receive it, it will help you.

Hopefully, after reading this booklet and meditating on some of the truths I've shared, you are ready to exercise your authority as a believer in Jesus Christ. What Satan stole from Adam and Eve has been taken back by Jesus through His death, burial, and resurrection—and then He gave it to us.

It's time for us to start releasing our authority and keep the devil under our feet where he belongs!

If you enjoyed this booklet and would like to learn more about some of the things I've shared, I suggest you get the full teaching of *The Believer's Authority* in book form, study guide, DVD or CD album, or on a USB drive that contains audio and video recordings. You'll be blessed!

The truth will make you free (John 8:32), but it's only the truth you know that sets you free. What you don't know is hindering you. Dig deeper into the truth with these other teachings:

- *The Believer's Authority (full-length book)*
- *A Better Way to Pray*
- *Christian Philosophy*
- *What to Do When Your Prayers Seem Unanswered*
- *The Sovereignty of God*

These teachings are available either free of charge at **awmi.net/video**, **awmi.net/audio**, or for purchase in book, study guide, CD, DVD, or USB formats at **awmi.net/store**.

Receive Jesus as Your Savior

Choosing to receive Jesus Christ as your Lord and Savior is the most important decision you'll ever make!

God's Word promises, *"That if thou shalt confess with thy mouth the Lord Jesus, and shalt believe in thine heart that God hath raised him from the dead, thou shalt be saved. For with the heart man believeth unto righteousness; and with the mouth confession is made unto salvation"* (Rom. 10:9–10). *"For whosoever shall call upon the name of the Lord shall be saved"* (Rom. 10:13). By His grace, God has already done everything to provide salvation. Your part is simply to believe and receive.

Pray out loud: "Jesus, I acknowledge that I've sinned and need to receive what you did for the forgiveness of my sins. I confess that You are my Lord and Savior. I believe in my heart that God raised You from the dead. By faith in Your Word, I receive salvation now. Thank You for saving me."

The very moment you commit your life to Jesus Christ, the truth of His Word instantly comes to pass in your spirit. Now that you're born again, there's a brand-new you!

Please contact us and let us know that you've prayed to receive Jesus as your Savior. We'd like to send you some free materials to help you on your new journey. Call our Helpline: **719-635-1111** (available 24 hours a day, seven days a week) to speak to a staff member who is here to help you understand and grow in your new relationship with the Lord.

Welcome to your new life!

Receive the Holy Spirit

As His child, your loving heavenly Father wants to give you the supernatural power you need to live a new life. *"For every one that asketh receiveth; and he that seeketh findeth; and to him that knocketh it shall be opened… how much more shall your heavenly Father give the Holy Spirit to them that ask him?"* (Luke 11:10–13).

All you have to do is ask, believe, and receive! Pray this: "Father, I recognize my need for Your power to live a new life. Please fill me with Your Holy Spirit. By faith, I receive it right now. Thank You for baptizing me. Holy Spirit, You are welcome in my life."

Some syllables from a language you don't recognize will rise up from your heart to your mouth (1 Cor. 14:14). As you speak them out loud by faith, you're releasing God's power from within and building yourself up in the spirit (1 Cor. 14:4). You can do this whenever and wherever you like.

It doesn't really matter whether you felt anything or not when you prayed to receive the Lord and His Spirit. If you believed in your heart that you received, then God's Word promises you did. *"Therefore I say unto you, What things soever ye desire, when ye pray, believe that ye receive* them, *and ye shall have* them" (Mark 11:24). God always honors His Word—believe it!

We would like to rejoice with you, pray with you, and answer any questions to help you understand more fully what has taken place in your life!

Please contact us to let us know that you've prayed to be filled with the Holy Spirit and to request the book *The New You & the Holy Spirit*. This book will explain in more detail about the benefits of being filled with the Holy Spirit and speaking in tongues. Call our Helpline: **719-635-1111** (available 24 hours a day, seven days a week).

Call for Prayer

If you need prayer for any reason, you can call our Helpline, 24 hours a day, seven days a week at **719-635-1111**. A trained prayer minister will answer your call and pray with you.

Every day, we receive testimonies of healings and other miracles from our Helpline, and we are ministering God's nearly-too-good-to-be-true message of the Gospel to more people than ever. So, I encourage you to call today!

About the Author

Andrew Wommack's life was forever changed the moment he encountered the supernatural love of God on March 23, 1968. As a renowned Bible teacher and author, Andrew has made it his mission to change the way the world sees God.

Andrew's vision is to go as far and deep with the Gospel as possible. His message goes far through the *Gospel Truth* television program, which is available to over half the world's population. The message goes deep through discipleship at Charis Bible College, headquartered in Woodland Park, Colorado. Founded in 1994, Charis has campuses across the United States and around the globe.

Andrew also has an extensive library of teaching materials in print, audio, and video. More than 200,000 hours of free teachings can be accessed at **awmi.net**.

Endnotes

1. *Vine's Expository Dictionary of New Testament Words*, s.v. "wiles," accessed February 7, 2023, https://www.blueletterbible.org/search/Dictionary/viewTopic.cfm?topic=VT0003343

2. Charles Capps, "Decrees: Their Force & Power," Harrison House, Accessed Feb. 7, 2023, https://harrisonhouse.com/blog/charles-capps-decrees-their-force-and-power

3. Kenneth E. Hagin, *The Triumphant Church*, Broken Arrow, OK: Faith Library Publications, 1993 (Sixth Printing, 1996), 59.

Contact Information

Andrew Wommack Ministries, Inc.

PO Box 3333
Colorado Springs, CO 80934-3333
info@awmi.net
awmi.net

Helpline: 719-635-1111 (available 24/7)

Charis Bible College

info@charisbiblecollege.org
844-360-9577
CharisBibleCollege.org

For a complete list of all of our offices,
visit **awmi.net/contact-us**.

Connect with us on social media.